Spooky Schools

ian Moses lives in a small Sussex village with his wife
d their two daughters. He travels the UK and the
ntinent, presenting poetry and percussion shows in
ools and libraries. He understands what spooky places
ools can be because he was a teacher (in a previous
arnation!) and on dark nights when he stayed late at
ool, it would be his responsibilty to go round and turn off
he lights before exiting the building . . . very rapidly!

Long, long ago,
In a dark and dingy crypt,
There lay a book of writings,
In a strange and ancient script,
It tells a tale of evil,
Oh so ghastly and so foul,
To listen once is fair enough,
But more will make you howl!
It tells you of a man, you see,
Whose name you're sure to learn,
The Doctor Death of Illustration,
Sinister Sam Hearn!

Other books from Macmillan

SPOOKY JOKES, PUZZLES AND POEMS

Sandy Ransford and David Orme

BEWARE OF THE DINNER LADY!

poems chosen by Brian Moses

THE SECRET LIVES OF TEACHERS

poems chosen by Brian Moses

THE TEACHER'S REVENGE

poems chosen by Brian Moses

SPECTACULAR SCHOOLS

poems chosen by Paul Cookson and David Harmer

Spooky Schools

poems chosen by
Brian Moses

Illustrated by
Sam Hearn

MACMILLAN CHILDREN'S BOOKS

For Jo Collins & Sandra D'Warte
(Two scary teachers!!!)
with thanks

First published 2004 by Macmillan Children's Books
a division of Macmillan Publishers Limited
20 New Wharf Road, London N1 9RR
Basingstoke and Oxford
www.panmacmillan.com

Associated companies throughout the world

ISBN 0 330 41358 9

1 3 5 7 9 8 6 4 2

A CIP catalogue record for this book is available from
the British Library.

Typeset by Nigel Hazle
Printed and bound in Great Britain by Mackays of Chatham plc, Kent

Contents

Who Wants to Go to a New School Anyway? –
  Frances Nagle   1
It Could Be You – *Eric Finney*   2
Midnight on Mayday – *Mark Halliday*   5
The New Girl – *Clare Bevan*   6
Bob Bodge – *Liz Brownlee*   8
Mistress Malice's Witch School – *Marian Swinger*   10
A Vampire Teacher – *Marian Swinger*   14
Timetable – *Julia Rawlinson*   16
Ghoul School – *Danielle Sensier*   18
Skeleton Staff – *Mike Johnson*   19
A Breach of School Rules – *Trevor Harvey*   19
Nothing Scares Me – Much – *Patricia Leighton*   20
Beware the Ghoul's Lunch Box – *Lucinda Jacob*   22
Finishing Schools for Ghosts and Ghouls –
  Celia Warren   24
School Song of Grisly School – *Cynthia Rider*   26
Learning to Be a Ghost – *John Mole*   28
Our Headmaster – *Penny Kent*   29
Haunted Schools – *John Cotton*   30
The Phantom Fiddler – *Brian Moses*   31
The Teacher's Spook Speaks – *Wes Magee*   34
Clean Round the Bend – *Bill Longley*   35
Quieter than Snow – *Berlie Doherty*   36
Dinner Lady – *Peter Dixon*   38
Stop! Children Crossing (Or Else) – *Mike Johnson*   40
Substitute Teacher – *Douglas Florian*   42

The Ghoul Inspectre's Coming – *Liz Brownlee*   43

At the School of Weird Behaviour – *Trevor Harvey*   44

Miss Smith's Mythical Bag – *Paul Cookson*   46

The School that Followed Me Home – *David Bateman*   48

Wish a Wish – *Moira Andrew*   50

Out at Lunch – *Dave Calder*   52

School for Spiders – *Jan Dean*   54

A School to Send Shivers Down Your Spine – *Patricia Leighton*   56

The Beast in the Boiler House – *Wes Magee*   58

Classroom Ghost – *Lucinda Jacob*   62

The Ghoul School Bus – *Brian Moses*   63

Schooldays End – *Mandy Coe*   66

Is there a Ghost in this Classroom? – *Dave Calder*   68

The Cupboard – *Liz Brownlee*   70

The Cannibal Canteen Menu – *Damian Harvey*   72

The Horrible Headmonster – *Wes Magee*   74

The Haunted School – *Marian Swinger*   75

School Prospectus – *Alison Chisholm*   76

Caterwaul – *Clare Bevan*   78

Changing Rooms – *Gina Douthwaite*   80

Spooky Hill Night School – *Patricia Leighton*   82

Skeleton in the Cupboard – *Gina Douthwaite*   84

Another Art Lesson Where I Draw a House and Garden – *John Coldwell*   86

The Mummy Teacher Unwrap – *Roger Stevens*   88

Supplyclops – *Paul Cookson*   90

Who Wants to Go to a New School Anyway?

To get a place at Spooky Towers
You swot and swot for hours
And cram for their exam.

I was wizard at the theory, did it fine – ten out of nine.
But when it came to *The Magick Art*
I fell apart.

Instead of changing a vase of flowers
Into a hat, I turned a rather fierce invigilator
Into an alligator.

He didn't think much of that;
Got pretty snappy in fact.
Well he can keep his Spooky Towers

It's snobby and expensive, and besides
I rather think I'm happy where I am
At St Poltergeist's Comprehensive.

Frances Nagle

It Could Be You

The Finger came to school about a month ago:
came out of the air, out of nowhere.
No body, no arm even, just a big hand
with a pointing finger, hanging in the air.
And even as the head or our teacher
talked about them – the bullies, the graffiti artists,
the pests and pains-in-the-neck –
The Finger moved about and pointed at them.
It scared everyone witless at first,
this ghostly, disembodied hand,
but as we got used to it only the hooligans
feared it because, well, it put the finger on them.
After a while it began writing too
and proved to have a sense of humour:
our teacher, Mr Benbow, well known
for his grumpiness and bad temper,
was doing one of his tantrums when
The Finger appeared above him.
In the air, in a misty kind of handwriting
it wrote
　　　Ratbag!
The Finger and the writing faded quite quickly
but everyone saw it – including Benbow.
I don't think he's been quite so ratty since.
Above Mrs Kirkham, who's everyone's favourite
teacher, it wrote
　　　Sweetheart

one day and over my pal Baz, who's always
doing good things quietly, it wrote
    Nice Guy.
He went red with embarrassment
but you could tell he was pleased.
I suppose you could say it was
all a bit creepy, but anyway,
it's gone now – moving on, I suppose.
Keep a lookout – it might come to your school.

Eric Finney

Midnight on Mayday

When the church bell tolls farewell
to the first day of May,
and the milky, midnight moon
paints the playground frosty grey,
you can hear the snapped-stick clicking
of dusty, brittle bones as
forgotten pupils from centuries ago
climb out of their cold, churchyard plots.
Silently, they make their way down the hill,
push on the old school gate and rattle and scrape
towards the centre of the empty playground.
Slowly, in the loneliness, they start to dance
round the memory of a Maypole,
getting faster and faster,
the wind rushing right through them
as they skip, leap and dash to their places.
They end in a circle, ribcages heaving,
and stand for a time clutching each other
like the bare strands of an old funeral wreath.
Finally, they turn to share frozen smiles,
as if to say 'Now . . .
that's how it should be done!'

Mark Halliday

The New Girl

The new girl stood at Miss Moon's desk,
Her face pale as a drawing
On white paper,
Her lips coloured too heavily
With a too-dark crayon.

When the others shouted, 'Me! Me!'
I curled my fists,
Tried not to think of friendship,
Or whispered secrets,
Or games for two players.
But the empty seat beside me
Shimmered with need
And my loneliness dragged her like a magnet.

As she sat down
I caught the musty smell of old forests,
Noticed the threads that dangled
At her thin wrists,
The purple stitches that circled
Her swan's neck.
Yet I loved her quietness,
The way she held her pencil
Like a feather,
The swooping curves of her name,
The dreaminess of her cold eyes.

At night, I still wonder
Where she sleeps,
If she sleeps,
And what Miss Moon will say
To her tattered parents
On Open Day.

Clare Bevan

Bob Bodge

Magic Academy
Spellycoat Castle
Elfarrow
The North

Dear Ma,

Help! I'm not a wizard wizard, I'm embarrassingly bad —
I made our wiz-professor cry and wizard-master mad.
My spells and magic potions all go wrong — it's very weird,
My pill to make me disappear — instead IT disappeared!
My sleeping potion fell asleep and snored all though the
　　lesson —
My devilish curse got scruples and suffered with
　　depression.
My love draught fell in love with me and sent me slurpy
　　kisses
and my indigestion cure made disgusting burps and
　　hisses.
Levitation worked *too* well, my frog stuck to the ceiling.
Worst, Mum, please come quickly, if you have any feeling,

8

my truth spell told the truth to the wizard-head today —
that he's ugly as a bowl of toads — which is why I've run
   away.

Please meet me at the wyching gate,
tomorrow noon — AND DON'T BE LATE,
if I'm caught I'll be in such a fix,
tomorrow's lesson's GYMBROOMSTICKS!

Bob X

Liz Brownlee

Mistress Malice's Witch School

Motto: *Have broomstick, will travel.*

TIMETABLE FOR TUESDAY

9 a.m. Assembly
Appeals to the Great Goddess.
Live sacrifices unnecessary,
the Great Goddess is vegetarian.
A ritually slaughtered carrot will do nicely.

9.30 a.m. Wart Charms
A must in every witch's repertoire.
All young ladies at this establishment
are expected to have at least three warts
on the end of the nose.
Prettiness is not permitted.

10.15 a.m. Love Potions. Mixing and application
It is forbidden to try these out on Wizard School pupils.
Your Head, Mistress Malice, will not have wizardlets
singing serenades underneath the boarders' dormitories.

11 a.m. Break
Do not curse your playground attendants.
When you misbehave, they turn you into frogs for your
    own good.
The young lady who cursed Mistress Wrath with a plague of
        man-eating fleas was most misguided,
but congratulations on a jolly good curse, all the same.
11.30 a.m. Flying Practice

Do NOT bring high-powered broomsticks to this class.
Poor Mother Dread had six pupils launch into space last
   week.
It is too much for her at her age (210).
Besides, the young ladies in question are still in orbit
and their parents won't give Mistress Malice a moment's
   peace.

12.30 p.m. Lunch
One meat and two veg as usual.
Those who do not eat their greens will be cursed.
When in the playground, do not taunt the wizardlets
in the Wizard's School playground, so annoyingly opposite
   ours
The playground is pitted with craters from all the misfired
   spells.
Poor Grudge, the caretaker, was dragged into one
by what appeared to be a great purple spotted, triple-horned
   demon
from the twenty-third dimension, and hasn't been seen
   since.

1.30 p.m. Transmogrification

Changing a human into one of the lesser beasts.

It is forbidden to change classmates into anything larger
than a cat

Since the badly behaved Tabitha Titmuss changed
Grizelda Inch into an elephant.

It was very naughty of Grizelda to sit upon six of her
enemies

and the consequent loss of school fees grieved Mistress
Malice greatly.

2.30 p.m. Evil Eye Studies
Dark glasses MUST be worn to prevent inadvertent Evil
Eye casting.
Last year, Mistress Trout withered away right in front of her
class
and all because of an unguarded evil eye.
Several young ladies fainted, but that was no help to
Mistress Trout.

3 p.m. Cauldron practice
Bring your own graveyard dew and don't forget your black
cats.
There have been too many tabby cats turning up lately.
These are NOT school uniform and will be sent home.

3.30 p.m. Home time for day girls
Parents are reminded not to clog the entrance with their
broomsticks.
This had led to broomstick rage on several occasions lately
and has been an extremely bad example to the young
ladies.

Those of you who are boarders are reminded that we
expect you up and about at midnight, under the full moon,
in the haunted graveyard, collecting materials for your
spells. Those found snoring in bed at this time will lose
house points.

Marian Swinger

A Vampire Teacher

Last night I saw our teacher,
a pale, thin, corpse-like bloke
creeping round the churchyard
looking furtive, in a cloak.
He sat upon a gravestone
and he mumbled, 'Let me see,
to change into a bat
one simply murmurs, one two three.'
I saw a purple glimmer
and I heard a muffled bang
and just before he vanished,
a glimpse of gleaming fang.
Then, fluttering round the gravestone
where Mr Meek had sat
was a rather thin example
of the lesser vampire bat.
Next morning, in the classroom,
Mr Meek looked plump and pink.
Today I may buy garlic
and a crucifix I think.

Marian Swinger

Timetable

First-year ghosts, 9 p.m.,
First class, 'Elementary Moaning',
10 p.m. at local churchyard,
'Get to Grips with Graveyard Groaning',
10.30, practical,
'How to Remove your Head',

12 midnight, back to churchyard,
'Seven Steps to Wake the Dead',
1 a.m., 'Dragging Chains',

2 a.m., 'Ringing Bells',
3 a.m., 'To Mix Fake Blood',
4 a.m., 'Revolting Smells',
5 a.m., dawn instruction,
'Murky Mists and Spooky Lighting',

5.30, theory class,
'The Basics of Successful Frightening',
6 a.m., lost property,
Please reclaim your missing head,
6.30, class dismissed,
Vanish, fade or float to bed.

Julia Rawlinson

Ghoul School

I want to go to ghoul school
I want to learn to trick poor unsuspecting humans
I want to make them shriek
I want to make them tremble
I want to make them shake
It's time I learnt the secrets of how to shift my shape
I need the latest recipe for human casserole
When can I go to ghoul school, Mum
I'm bored to death at home

Danielle Sensier

Skeleton Staff

The local News reported that,
'Due to an outbreak of flu,
most schools will have a skeleton staff.'
I'm not going today – are you?

Mike Johnson

A Breach of School Rules

'WHY are you here?'
The teacher frowned.
'Spectres AREN'T ALLOWED
In the GHOULS' Playground!'

Trevor Harvey

Nothing Scares Me
— Much

There's a skeleton
Skulking in the games store?
Doesn't rattle me.

A hairy werewolf
Haunts the hall?
Tell me more.

A zombie's cornered
The caretaker in the corridor?
What are we waiting for?

A witch and a warlock
Are spelling the head bright blue?
What's new.

A phantom's hanging about
On one of the cloakroom pegs?
How many legs?

A ghost, a ghoul and a poltergeist
Are trashing the school kitchen?
Who are you kidding!

A yeti
With machete teeth
And blood-red jaws
Is smashing down
The classroom door?
Is that all?

Miss Phipps is after me
For last night's homework?
LET ME OUT OF HERE!

Patricia Leighton

Beware The Ghoul's Lunch Box

Look in a vampire's lunch box;
       Lift the lid if you can
       On a dripping scream bun
       Filled with bloodberry jam.

Look in a witch's lunch box
       And try not to sneeze
       Over snail-shell crackers
       Flavoured with fleas.

Look in a ghost's lunch box;
       You can eat if you're dead
       A see-through mist sandwich
       Made from barely-there bread.

Look in a wizard's lunch box;
       If you're crazy you'll find
       Fizzy-drink fireworks
       To alter your mind.

Look in a goblin's lunch box;
       This might make you wheeze:
       It's slime jelly – flavoured
       With stings of dead bees.

Look in a banshee's lunch box;
     You'll shiver with cold
     If you taste the mice-cream
     With a smear of green mould.

But beware the ghoul's lunch box!
     It's shaped like a tomb
     There's lots of us in here
     There's plenty of room!

Lucinda Jacob

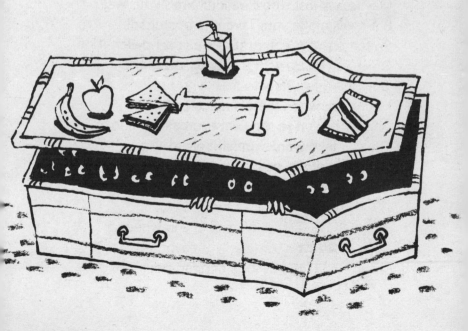

Finishing Schools for Ghosts and Ghouls

At finishing schools
For ghosts and ghouls
They learn to cope with the hassles
Of life without enough castles.
They practise rattling balls and chains,
Not in Great Halls, but down the drains.
There's even a high-tech tutor
Who explains how to haunt a computer.
So, when you lie in bed at night,
Feeling safe with your modern security light,
Maybe a ghost won't walk through your wall,
But it will make your favourite poster fall,
Switch on your computer when you switch it off
Or wake you up with a sudden cough.
They learn just how to freak you out;
Haunt you when there's no one about
And when you're reading, even as you look,
They'll make words vanish from your . . .
As taught at the best of finishing schools
Where all the students are ghosts and . . .

Celia Warren

School Song of Grisly School

(which, by an uncanny coincidence, can be sung to the tune of the Eton Boating Song)

Let's raise three haunting cheers
And sing with icy breath,
How our days at Grisly School
Are the very best days of our death.

Chorus: For we're all spooks together
              At the school for ghosts and ghouls
              And we're having the time of our death
              Obeying the Grisly rules.

Here in the echoing classrooms
Where cobwebs hang like lace,
We learn the art of scaring
The cowardly human race.

Chorus: For we're all spooks together . . .

We ride on the wings of midnight
And fill our foes with dread
By uttering bloodcurdling screeches
As we hover over their beds.

Chorus: For we're all spooks together . . .

So let's raise three haunting cheers
For the school that we adore,
For we're all convinced that Grisly
Is a school worth dying for.

Chorus: And we're all spooks together
         At the school for ghosts and ghouls
         And we're having the time of our death
         Obeying the Grisly rules.

Cynthia Rider

Learning to Be a Ghost

School is just the place for me
To practise after dark,
With no kids in the classrooms
And no cars in the park,
With stillness in the playground,
With silence in the hall,
Nothing to distract me,
No one there at all.

Perhaps a little moonlight
Spilling on the floor,
Perhaps some lurking shadows
Along the corridor,
Perhaps a not-quite-turned-off tap,
Perhaps a broken blind,
But drip-drip-drip and rattle
Are sounds I mustn't mind.

So this is where I teach myself
When everyone's gone home.
Until I've got the hang of it
I need to be on my own,
But as soon as I'm an expert,
As soon as I've learned to be
A confident and skilful ghost
then you'll be seeing me!

John Mole

Our Headmaster

patrols the corridors, shuffling by
unshaven and bent, hollow-cheeked, rheumy eyed,
with a mumble, a mutter, a patient sigh.

Like someone's old grandad he'll stop with a smile
to ask how you're doing, chat for a while
and pat your head in his gentle style.

His expression may seem genial and dim
but beware, if you're bad your chances are slim.
When his ire is aroused the results may be grim.

When bullies first come here they snigger and scoff
but we know that little testy cough;
we recognize that it's warning us off.

As many a wrongdoer can affirm,
he doesn't use strength to make you squirm
only somehow you writhe like an abject worm.

Three warnings and then he's had enough.
It's no good posturing, acting tough.
You'll just *disappear*
      in a faint,
          small
           puff.

Penny Kent

Haunted Schools

Has your school got ghosts?
Of pupils or staff long left and gone?
So if you go there at weekends or the holidays
And listen, in the quiet you can hear the faint echoes
Of past classes and the sounds of singing
And laughter in the hall.
You can detect them if you stand quietly enough,
And from the playground and the fields
The sounds of matches, sports days,
And general playtime shrieking,
And in your imagination the peaceful
Scratchy, breathy hush of work times.
Sounds never quite go away,
But they lurk and sulk lonely,
In small corners or high in the ceilings,
Waiting to be heard
By those who listen carefully enough.

John Cotton

The Phantom Fiddler

(A ghostly apparition said to haunt Thresfield School in the Dales)

There can't be an apparition
in our school.
We have rules to stop anyone
getting in.
We have keypads and an intercom
to keep children from harm.
Yet it seems that something
has invaded our building,
something that I heard last night
as I scooted down the street.
A screeching sound
like a fiddler playing,
laying down a curious tune
by the light of a magical moon,

And as I peered through the window,
into the gloom of 3B's room,
I caught a glimpse of children,
or were they imps,
dancing round to the sounds
a fiddler played.
And I had to admit
that the music captured me.
And I danced to the fiddler's tune
by the light of a magical moon.

Sensible people would have scuttled by,
they wouldn't have lingered like I did.
they wouldn't have looked in the fiddler's eye
or followed when he crooked his finger.
And I had no choice but to stay with him
as I danced to the tune he played,
and the imps came too
as we danced in the street
by the light of a magical moon.

But something must have broken the spell,
something must have woken me up.
And I saw the imps for what they were,
nasty, ghastly, horrid things
that chased me all the way to the well
where I leapt in the Holy Water.

* * * * * *

And that's where I was found
later that night,
when lights blazed over the hill,
shivering down in Lady's Well,
still hearing that phantom fiddler's tune
by the light of a magical moon.

Brian Moses

The Teacher's Spook Speaks . . .

For making me tear out my hair,
for drawing pins left on my chair,
for calling me Old Grizzly Bear
        I'll be spooking you . . .

For all the tiresome tricks you played,
for rotten stink-bomb smells you made,
for rank bad manners you displayed
        I'll be spooking you . . .

For rude things drawn on wall and door,
for muddy kit on cloakroom floor,
for all your ceaseless jaw jaw jaw
        I'll be spooking you . . .

For making fun of my big ears,
for playground spats that end in tears,
for all the headaches down the years
        I'll be spooking you . . .

For all who thought it fun to shout
or squeal or spit or clown or clout
you'd best beware, you'd best watch out
        for – yes indeed! –
        be in no doubt
        I'll be spooking you . . .

Wes Magee

34

Clean Round the Bend

People get some mad ideas;
Our head has more than most:
Instead of having cleaning staff
She's hired a cleaning ghost.

The school will stay securely locked,
As ghosts can walk through doors.
He won't leave marks of muddy feet
On newly polished floors.

A ladder isn't needed now;
He simply floats around
To clean the windows in the hall
High up off the ground.

We save on electricity:
He's used to working nights;
There isn't any need for him
To switch on any lights.

Above all, since the ghost's not real,
He doesn't need real pay.
Our head's idea is not so daft:
We save in every way.

Bill Longley

Quieter than Snow

I went to school a day too soon
And couldn't understand
Why silence hung in the yard like sheets
Nothing to flap or spin, no creaks
Or shocks of voices, only air.

And the car park empty of teachers' cars
Only the first September leaves
Dropping like paper. No racks of bikes
No kicking legs, no fights,
No voices, laughter, anything.

Yet the door was open. My feet
Sucked down the corridor. My reflection
Walked with me past the hall.
My classroom smelt of nothing. And the silence
rolled like thunder in my ears.

At every desk a still child stared at me
Teachers walked through walls and
            back again
Cupboard doors swung open, and out crept
More silent children, and still more.

They tiptoed round me
Touched me with ice-cold hands
And opened up their mouths with laughter
That was

Quieter than snow.

Berlie Doherty

Dinner Lady

Dinner lady, dinner lady,
     what do you do?
I serve out potatoes, cabbage and stew . . .
     I watch out for trouble
     and children who shout,
     knock over water
     or stamp on a sprout.
I catch naughty children
     to make into pies,
     boil with spaghetti
     or serve up with fries.
I spread them on pizzas,
     I curry them too,
     bake with bananas
     or flavour the stew.
I roast them with olives
     or rosemary leaf,
     grill them with bacon
     or broil them with beef.
I even make sarnies
     garnished with boys,
     sprinkled with infants
     or small saveloys.

I really love cooking,
all children are nice
covered with pastry
and served up with rice.

Peter Dixon

Stop! Children Crossing (Or Else)

Yes, she may seem hideous and gruesome,
but all we children think she's 'Awesome!'
Out she'll step, a fearsome sight;
would give King Kong a spiteful fright.
Her speciality is chilling blood,
makes waiting drivers faint – bonk, thud! –
with fangs that are spectacular.
They'd be at home on Dracula:
OK, she could be his best mate;
but all we children think she's 'Great!'
Her hairstyle writhes, like deadly snakes
(no wonder truckers hit their brakes).
One eye looks up, the other down
and both start turning round and round,
a stare that could turn you to stone.
You should hear her wail and moan.
She might get the part as Frankenstein's bride,
but she's so cool – and on our side.
She belches smoke, dear Gorgon's breath
has scared three policemen half to death.
Whatever planet saw her birth,
no way was it Planet Earth,
for if this vision fills with dread,
you should see her *other* head.
Yes, she may seem hideous and gruesome,
but all we children think she's 'Awesome!'

Mike Johnson

Substitute Teacher

Today we had a substitute.
She wasn't sweet.
She wasn't cute.
Her hair could scare a ghastly ghost.
Her breath could turn bread into toast.
She barely fit inside the door
And looked much like a dinosaur.
Each time she spoke the windows shook,
And when she read she broke the book.
She didn't have a lesson plan
But walked like an orang-utan.
And if someone would misbehave,
Her screams could start a tidal wave.
But if you think that SHE'S a creature,
Wait till you meet our REGULAR teacher.

Douglas Florian

The Ghoul Inspectre's Coming

The Ghoul
Inspectre's coming,
dust off your lazy bones —
tidy out your coffins, polish
up your mournful moans.
Practise rib-cage rattles,
check that your chains still clank, gibber when you're
spoken to and keep your cellars dank. Display your
bat collection and cobweb-hanging talents —
freshen up the bloodstains, see
that the spook books balance.
Hover to attention, grease
your glides and brush
your mould — the
Ghoul Inspectre's
coming, make
sure his
welcome's
Cold!

Liz Brownlee

At the School of Weird Behaviour
(A staff meeting, not for the faint-hearted!)

The teachers are holding a meeting
Chaired by the Caretaker's Cat –
And Mrs McClaw (who teaches class four)
Has hung upside down, like a bat;
Young Mr Court (who takes mainly sport)
Is crouching down low, like a toad;
And the head, Mrs Pheasant, is sounding unpleasant
(when she opened her mouth she just crowed).

Miss Skinner's amiss; she does nothing but 'hiss'
As she slithers about on the floor;
And old Mr Pailing is certainly ailing –
He keeps fading from sight, by the door!
Mrs O'Grady, the classroom-help lady,
Has been hopping about, in a daze –
And poor Mrs Brunch (who just 'helps out' at lunch)
Has dropped fourteen plates and ten trays!

Miss Pane has jumped out through the window –
Miss Pinkerton's face has turned red;
Mr Flyman has walked on the ceiling –
Miss Downside has stood on her head!

The reason? It's perfectly simple –
I'm certain you'll see the connection;
NO WONDER the teachers act SCARY!
The school has just FAILED an inspection!

Trevor Harvey

Miss Smith's Mythical Bag

The curse of every class she'll see
No one knows its history
Its origin's a mystery
. . . Miss Smith's Mythical Bag.

Beyond our understanding
You dare not put your hand in
The bag that keeps expanding
. . . Miss Smith's Mythical Bag.

Broken chalk, a thousand pens with red ink that's
    congealed,
Forgotten fungus-covered bread with mouldy orange peel,
Lost car keys and headache pills, a Roman spear and
    shield,
Football cards and marbles, the goalposts from the field.

Where she goes it follows
All rippling lumps and hollows
The strangest things it swallows
. . . Miss Smith's Mythical Bag.

With a menacing unzipped grin it's
From the Outer Limits
There are black holes deep within it
. . . Miss Smith's Mythical Bag.

Crinkled tissues, Blu-tack balls, disfigured paper clips,
Sweets all covered up with fluff, dried up fibre-tips,
Lumps of powdered milk and coffee, last year's fish and
   chips,
From the Triangle in Bermuda — several missing ships.

Sometimes you hear it groan
Beyond the Twilight Zone
Make sure you're not alone
. . . Miss Smith's Mythical Bag.

Shape-shifting, changing sizes,
The bag she never tidies,
It metamorphosizes
. . . Miss Smith's Mythical Bag.

More mysterious than Loch Ness, it's from the Fifth
   Dimension.
Stranger than an alien race beyond our comprehension.
Brooding with a strange intent that no one wants to
   mention
You'd better pay attention or you'll be in detention.

With Miss Smith's mythical, metaphysical,
astronomical, gastronomical, anatomical
clinical, cynical bag!

Paul Cookson

The School that Followed Me Home

I'm walking out the gate from school
And hear an eerie sound
– A creaky, crunchy sort of noise –
But don't dare look around.

Then as I'm riding on the bus
I hear the noise behind,
But still I don't dare turn my head
For fear of what I'll find.

And *still*, while walking up my road
I hear the scraping roar:
That dreadful sound still follows me
Right up to my front door.

And when at last I turn around,
What's happened is quite plain.
That wretched school is sitting there:
It's followed me *again*!

The school is meant to stay at school.
It isn't meant to roam.
I don't know why it follows me.
We don't want it at home.

I know that empty schools at night
Must lead quite lonely lives;
But this one's filling up our road,
And blocking neighbours' drives.

And though I don't mind cats and dogs
That wander down our way,
Head teachers should take much more care
So that their schools don't stray.

But every afternoon I'm forced
To phone up and complain:
'Your wretched school's outside my door!
It's followed me *again*!'

David Bateman

Wish a Wish

I'll never make the top group, I'm rotten at
loads of things, no good at maths or music,
hopeless on sports days – I'm always last.
But I've got one secret talent, I'm brilliant
      at making wishes come true.

The caretaker stared up at a ball out of reach,
grunted, 'If only I could fly!' I wrinkled my nose,
and blinked three times. He rose into the sky
on scarlet wings, drifted down to get the ball,
      a puzzled expression on his face.

Then there was the head. 'I wish I had a pound
for every time I've asked you lot to be quiet,'
she said. I did my nose-wrinkling eye-blinking
routine and a hail of newly minted pound coins
      rattled down around her feet.

A hot day in the kitchen, dinner ladies sweating
under their silly hats. 'I wish these potatoes
would learn to peel themselves,' I heard one say.
I wrinkled and blinked and a whole bag of Maris
      Pipers tumbled naked into the bowl.

'What on earth's going on?' they asked one another.
'I wish we knew.' I tried not to wrinkle my nose, not
to blink, but I'd got into the habit by now. So I wished
myself invisible and vanished into thin air. 'Where
has that girl got to?' I heard them ask.

But it's my secret and I'm not telling.

Moira Andrew

Out at Lunch

All morning the rain had gobbed on the windows
and going over to lunch we all got soaked so that
you could hardly see the room for the steam rising
from wet clothes and wide tins of food and what
with the dank overpowering smells and the flu coming on
my head was swimming and as we're standing in this mist,
in line with our trays, JJ behind me says, 'Look
worms in blood again,' and though I knew he meant
the spaghetti I got this uneasy sensation
that the white mass was twitching, but I felt so unsteady
I said nothing. It was like being inside a cloud,
not floating although my legs no longer felt sure
they were part of me and JJ's face seemed to swell
and his voice was at once far away and very loud,
'Look, cat stew, you can see bits of fur, cat spew stew,
look, green sheep droppings, and is that maggots in rice
or rice in the maggots . . .' There was no stopping him
when he'd started this game, I tell you, one time he'd
put string in his curry and insisted it was a rat's tail
long after it was funny. 'Hey, I'd like some baked bugs
   please,
with mashed brains and a giant slug.' My knees
were wobbly, I took a cheese roll and an orange juice
and even they seemed too much. When we sat down I felt
   worse,
I couldn't touch the food, I stared at the table, at the usual
crumbs, stains and slops, at JJ's plate opposite. Most
of all at his plate for it seemed like the beans

were squirming and one or two slid off, over the rim,
and scuttled away. It was a bit odd but I was past caring,
I felt like I was hanging over a huge pit, head spinning
so everything around was distant and dim
except for JJ's blether, now a meaningless babble
of surging waves through the blurring mist
and his left fist gripping a fork he'd just jabbed
into the mound of pale mashed potato
that looked strangely like I thought my brain felt inside my
     head
and when with a slow slither
the sausage twisted sideways and bit into his wrist
I fainted.

Dave Calder

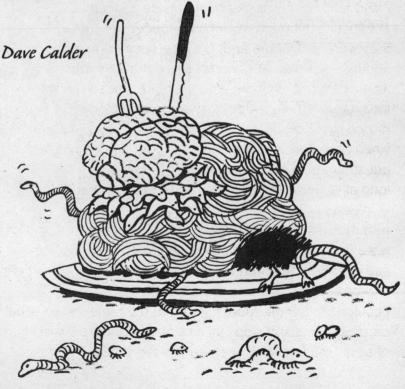

School for Spiders — Timetable

Monday

Spin and spin
Spin thread
So thin
That eyes can't
see it
Till it's too late
Spin and spin
Until
The victim's
Trapped within . . .

Tuesday

Run and scuttle
Shuttle back and
forth
For all you're
worth.
Flit and skitter like
a crazy black dot
Leggy black spot
Murky blood clot

Websday

Suddenly
Where once
was space,
There's web.
You know I'm
here.
But you can't
see me
I'm your secret
fear.

Thursday

Is hanging day.
Is dangling day.
Is angling from
the light shade,
Like a shadow,
Like a drop
of deadly
nightshade.

Frightday

Is anything you
like day.
So long as it's
scary
Wriggly, black
and hairy.

On weekends we get time off
For fun – a break from working
So Saturdays and Sundays
We chill out and do *lurking*.

Jan Dean

A School to Send Shivers Down Your Spine!

Imagine a school
        where no one was ever late
        through the gate, where everyone
        reached every lesson spot on time
        (including the teachers).

Imagine a school
        where boys never fought
        no girls were ever catty;
        batty teachers were barred
        and caretakers rescued
        lost balls from gutters
        without one 'please' being uttered.

Imagine a school
        where each member of staff
        was sweetness and light
        from the first bell to the last;
        where the head
        cut no one down to size
        with a scary aside, a look like ice,
        or a mega-decibel blast of the vocal chords.

Imagine a school
　　　　where absolute peace and quiet
　　　　was the norm every day, every hour;
　　　　where no jokes or notes broke
　　　　into 'heads down' hard work;
　　　　where no ties were askew
　　　　all shoes polished
　　　　trainers never worn
　　　　ears remained unpierced
　　　　hair was shiny and combed
　　　　and sweatshirts worn neatly
　　　　(even on the way home).

A school of
　　　　no bags missing
　　　　no secret kissing
　　　　no gum on the yard
　　　　no cards to swop
　　　　no litter, no pop.

A school
　　　　where not a single pencil or pen
　　　　was ever lost –

　　　　Scary, or what!

Patricia Leighton

The Beast in the Boiler House

There's a huddle on the playground,
dozen pupils — maybe more,
all ear-wigging John-Paul's story
about what he heard and saw
when he ventured down the stone steps
to the Boiler House's door.

'I found an old key in the lock.
It was really thick with rust
and when the door creaked opened,
wow, a t'rific pong of must!
I stepped inside and saw the place
was carpeted with dust.'

John-Paul paused
and scratched his nose.
'What happened next?'
asked Rachel Rose.
       And
          the huddled heads
              drew
                 closer . . .

'The Boiler House was dark and hot.
My heart went boom-de-boom
when I heard the huge machinery
throb-throbbing in the gloom.
And then . . . I saw a "thing" arise
like a zombie from its tomb!'

John-Paul stopped
and tugged his ear,
'What happened next?'
breathed Bully Beer.
And
the huddled heads
drew
closer . . .

'A huge Beast lumbered forward.
Around its head buzzed flies.
Its matted fur coat crawled with lice
and it had *three* bloodshot eyes.
It reached out with a warty hand
to grab my arm. No lies!'

John-Paul coughed
and itched his chin.
'What happened next?'
gasped Tracey Thin.
And
the huddled heads
drew
closer,
closer . . .

'It gave a snarl. I turned and ran!
I heard it give a snotty sneeze.
I belted up the steep stone steps,
fell *there*, and grazed my knees.
I'm telling you, that scary Beast
would make your hot blood freeze!'

     A bell rang.
     The end of morning break.
     'Some story, that,'
     said Steven Steak.
       And
         the huddlers headed
           back to
             school.

As they passed the steep stone steps
they stopped and gazed in awe
at the trace of blood where John-Paul fell,
then looking downwards saw
the old key really thick with rust
in the Boiler House's door . . .

Wes Magee

Classroom Ghost

The ghost in our classroom
Sleeps most of the time
When we're talking or laughing
Or getting in line.

But when we are quiet
Like now when we're writing
You can hear the 'creak creak'
And then gnawing and biting.

It makes my hand shake
And there's sweat on my face
The 'creak creak' makes my pen
Go all over the place.

'You can't possibly hear him,'
Our teacher said,
'I got rid of his cage,
You all know that he's dead.'

But his wheel keeps on creaking
And I hear his nails scrape
And I wish our ghost hamster
Could make an escape!

Lucinda Jacob

The Ghoul School Bus

The ghoul school bus
is picking up its cargo
of little horrors.

They must all be home
before first light, when today
turns into tomorrow.

All the sons and daughters of vampires,
little Igors and junior Fangs,
the teenage ghouls with their ghoulfriends
all wail, as the bus bell clangs.

And the driver doesn't look well,
he's robed completely in black,
and the signboard says — Transylvania,
by the way of hell and back.

The seats are slimy and wet,
there's a terrible graveyard smell,
all the small ghouls cackle and spit,
and practise their ghoulish spells.

The witches are reading their ABCs,
cackling over 'D' for disease,
while tomboy zombies are falling apart
and werewolves are checking for fleas.

When the bus slows down to drop them off
at Coffin Corner or Cemetery Gates,
their mummies are waiting to greet them
with eyes full of anguish and hate.

The ghoul school bus
is dropping off its cargo
of little horrors.

They must all be home
before first light, when today
turns into tomorrow.

Brian Moses

Schooldays End

When I was built, children walked
for miles, called by my iron bell.
No cars, electric light or felt-pens.
Just hurrying feet, the hiss of gas
and the squeal of chalk on slate.

They say that I am haunted now.
My attic creaks, twisted black gates
bang in the wind. A shadow-game
flickers across the yard. Now, the children
hurry past me to the new school. I see them

carrying their toys and picture books,
their lunch boxes and football boots.
The new school is warm and full of music,
its windows, bright with cut-out shapes.
Mine are dark and broken – they see no light.

This dark night is the last.
Moonlight spills down my slate roof.
I wish my bell could ring out again:
Come to me, children! Run! Run!
Tomorrow the bulldozers come.

Mandy Coe

Is there a Ghost in this Classroom?

Before anything, don't turn around,
ghosts are never where you expect them to be.
Let's look for signs. Does your desk lid
slam unexpectedly while you're carefully closing it?
Do pens and pencils wriggle and squirm,
slip from your fingers and dive to the floor?
And when you look for them, they've disappeared
and no one can find them for weeks and weeks
until they turn up dusty, under a radiator,
looking much the same but not feeling quite right?
Do the legs of your chair wobble nervously?
Do stacks of exercise books mysteriously slither apart
or your biro suddenly start to write in invisible ink?
And when you're working, do you sometimes sense
someone watching you – and it's not the teacher,
who's looking out of the window, or your friends,
who are watching their hands write – but
somewhere you can't see, but can feel like heat or light,
you know something's eyes are staring into you?

Now tell me, do you feel
A sudden small wind licking your ankles,
a slow cold shiver sliding up your leg?
Is there an icy itch prickling your neck?
Do you hear a soft whispering, so close and quiet
it sounds like it's inside your head?
You do?
Then there is a ghost in this classroom
and it's here
to haunt YOU.

Dave Calder

The Cupboard

There's a cupboard in our classroom,
which is where our teacher keeps
supplies like pens and paper.
It's very dark and very deep.

It's very dark and very dank,
and Miss won't go in alone —
but she says 'there's nothing in there'
and sends us in all on our own.

It's scary in there on your own,
for the walls are painted black.
There's a corner you can't see round
in the shadows at the back.

In the shadows round the corner,
something whispers, something whines.
Unearthly mirthless giggles send
chills up and down your spine.

You'll be chilled if Miss needs pencils,
as you creep in full of dread,
something taps you on the shoulder,
then it cuffs you round the head.

Then it raps you on the knuckles,
or swipes behind your knees,
something sinister and dreadful,
something that you cannot see.

'There's nothing there you cannot see,'
says our teacher, 'go on in!'
But something's screaming in there now –
our teacher is – we locked her in!

Liz Brownlee

The Cannibal Canteen Menu
Meals 'R' Us

(Serving a balanced diet of pupils past and present –
why not bring a friend)

Whet your appetite from our
Selection of Succulent Starters

Crunchy Scabs freshly baked
(They're virtually fat-free)

Crispy Ears done to perfection
(You can dunk them in your tea)

Belly buttons served on bed of fluff
(They're buy one get one free)

Followed by one of our
Magnificent Main Courses

The Head Boy's surprise
(A selection of the best brains in the school)

Rump Steak
(With finger rolls)

Knuckle Bones
(Freshly cracked)

Soft-boiled Nose
(Picked today)

All served with nail clippings and trimmings of hair
(Miss them if you dare)

Today's Special

Chef's Spare Ribs
(Don't miss these – because he won't)

Sweets and Desserts

Rice Pudding with Skin on

Jelly and Custard

(The Cannibal Canteen is an equal-opportunities employer
First come first served – as next week's main course)

Damian Harvey

The Horrible Headmonster

A new Headmaster arrives next week
    and rumours about him are rife.
They say he growls like a grizzly bear
    and that he chopped up his wife.

It's said he'll stride and stomp around school
    like a zombie in the night,
And that his icicle stare can freeze
    hundreds of children with fright.

It's rumoured he wears a skull-shaped ring,
    and a tie with nests of fleas.
When he smiles he shows razor-sharp fangs.
    There are tattoos on his knees.

We've heard that he has a werewolf's howl.
    There's a jagged scar on his cheek.
They say that he owns a whippy cane
    and that he'll use it next week.

Already he's called the 'The Headmonster'
    and some have named him 'The Ghoul'.
We'll soon find out if the rumours are true
    when he arrives at our school.

Wes Magee

The Haunted School

The old school is haunted; kids live in dread
of a horrible phantom, its eyes, bulbous red,
its shape, fat and mouldy, a bad-tempered ghoul,
appearing in classrooms all round the school.
It floats round the desks and it hovers above
those idle young brats that the teachers don't love.
It observes as they scratch, pick their noses and wriggle.
It wails as they chatter, throw rubbers and giggle,
then descends with a shriek as they quiver in fear
and gives them a whack and a clip round the ear.
'Do better next time,' it groans, 'Try harder, do,'
and vanishes, leaving their hairstyles askew.
Parents, quite angry, cry, 'Call in a priest,
exorcize, spiflicate, banish the beast.'
But at times, in the staffroom, when teachers sip tea,
a grim, ghostly voice booms out, 'Save some for me.'
The teachers wink merrily; some start to laugh.
Get rid of their phantom! It's one of the staff.

Marian Swinger

School Prospectus

ST VLAD'S PRINCIPAL: DR H. JEKYLL

Founded in Transylvania in 1402,
this school caters for the sons
of gentlemen and the undead.

Boys are accommodated in dormitories
– in the charge of a house-mummy with good bandaging
   skills –
equipped with narrow but comfortable box beds.

Classes are conducted from sundown to sunrise,
and our extensive curriculum covers arithmetic,
alchemy, dragonology, ghoulonometry
and basic language studies in Latin and Early Ogre.

St Vlad's encourages sporting endeavour,
and werewolf hurdling, zombie chases
and griffon racing are popular among the boys.

There are extensive grounds, and our botany club
is proud of its fungus farm. Homing bats
roost in their loft, and the lake boasts
a fine school of giant water serpents.

Catering services are provided
by Guzzling Goblins incorporated, who guarantee
only the plumpest cockroaches are found in their pies.

So bring your little monsters and pay us a call.
Our qualified staff are dying to meet you.

Alison Chisholm

Caterwaul

Who yowls from the rooftops
Harsh and flat?
It's the mournful ghost
Of the Caretaker's Cat.

Who prowls the corridors
Pit-a-pat?
It's the faithful ghost
Of the Caretaker's Cat.

Who scratches his claws down
Board and bat?
It's the angry ghost
Of the Caretaker's Cat.

Who snatches the cheese from
Mouse and rat?
It's the hungry ghost
Of the Caretaker's Cat.

Who sleeps by the boiler
Coiled and fat?
It's the cosy ghost
Of the Caretaker's Cat.

Who creeps round our feet?
(I'm sure of that!)
It's the lonely ghost
Of the Caretaker's Cat.

Clare Bevan

Changing Rooms

Cloakrooms are bright, noisy places
with laughter and chatter, and faces
of friends having fun,
(though odd ones are glum)
and jackets and shoes,
lunch boxes and loos,
and water all over the floor
but that is what cloakrooms are for.

SHOUT!
but that is what cloakrooms are for.

Cloakrooms are creepy old places
when empty. They're like wire cages
with hissings and creaks
and breathing that speaks
and lone coats that hang
like each is a man
who's waiting to pounce when you pass.
At home time, try not to be last

OUT!
At home time, try not to be last.

Gina Douthwaite

Spooky Hill Night School

A school, a church, with a graveyard between;
From nine until four nothing strange is seen.
But when the sky's clock of glittering stars
Shows the witching hour, and a lone fox barks,
Skeletons stir beneath old stones
And rise from the earth with a shake of their bones.

They head for the school, form an orderly line,
And glide through locked doors, all dead on time
(Except for one who rattles in late,
His ghostly shirt hanging out at his waist).

Behind windows silvered with soft moonlight
They move down corridors, turn left and right
Into empty classrooms, eerie and grey,
Where the skeleton night school gets under way.

They scribble, scribble with phantom goose quills,
Slate chalk, biros, pencils and pens;
Skeleton pupils from down the ages
Filling up boards, filling up pages.

With skeletal grins on their skeleton faces,
With stars in their eyes (or at least, their eye spaces)
They chant their tables, spellings, read charts,
Sing songs, recite verses learned by heart.

Happy, contented, they work through the night
Till the moon slowly sinks and the dawn star brings light.
Then sighing and longing, wishing to stay,
How they envy the children's bright new day.

'*Someone should tell them*,' an old bag of bones
Croaks to his neighbour, who rises and moans
As they all wander out in fading waves,
Back to their tombstones, back to their graves.

'*Yes*,' says a voice, as it sinks below,
'*Someone should tell them
        that school days are
                the best . . .
                the best . . .
                        the best days of your life!*'

Patricia Leighton

Skeleton in the Cupboard

Miss Brittle's got a boyfriend,
a cupboard and a key,
she keeps him locked away in it
upon the balcony

but when it's time for Science
he's carried into class
their limbs entwined, her hand upon
his bony pelvic mass.

She indicates his carpus,
his clavicle and coccyx
while gazing like a lovesick girl
deep into his sockets.

She strokes his metacarpals,
runs fingers up his spine.
His mandible drops in a grin.
To Brittle he's divine

and when the bells fall silent
and endless daylight dims
they rattle round the balcony
and dance to haunting hymns.

Gina Douthwaite

Another Art Lesson Where I Draw a House and Garden

I don't like Art so first I coloured the sky
A deep, deep grey to help the time pass by.
But a ghostly notice began to appear
On my paper that said, 'Dracula was here.'
With trembling fingers I started to shade
The grass revealing a blood-dripping blade.
And amongst my scribbles across the lawn,
The message – 'You'll wish you had never been born.'
I dropped the green and began the roof instead
But across the slates the words emerged
   'Night of the living dead'.
My fingers shook with terror: I let the crayon fall
As ghostly figures materialized with no heads at all
From the dark clouds across my sky, streamed blood-red
   rain
On the heads of vicious goblins who writhed about in pain.

A bony hand from nowhere landed on my shoulder
The teacher who said, 'Make your picture strong and
   bolder.
Your house looks kind of spooky, but it's not quite right
Go for something to make me die of fright.'
I looked down at my picture with palpitating heart
The scary spooks had disappeared, which is why I hate Art.

John Coldwell